Posting on Social Media

JOSH GREGORY

Children's Press®
An Imprint of Scholastic Inc.

Content Consultant
Sarah Otts, Scratch Online Community Developer, MIT Media Lab

Library of Congress Cataloging-in-Publication Data
Names: Gregory, Josh.
Title: Posting on social media / by Josh Gregory.
Description: New York : Children's Press, 2019. | Series: A true book | Includes bibliographical references
    and index.
Identifiers: LCCN 2018021694| ISBN 9780531127346 (library binding) | ISBN 9780531135433 (pbk.)
Subjects: LCSH: Social media—Juvenile literature. | Online social networks—Juvenile literature.
Classification: LCC HM742 .G75 2019 | DDC 302.23/1—dc23
LC record available at https://lccn.loc.gov/2018021694

All rights reserved. Published in 2019 by Children's Press, an imprint of Scholastic Inc.
Printed in North Mankato, MN, USA 113

SCHOLASTIC, CHILDREN'S PRESS, A TRUE BOOK™, and associated logos are trademarks and/or
registered trademarks of Scholastic Inc.

Scholastic Inc., 557 Broadway, New York, NY 10012

1 2 3 4 5 6 7 8 9 10 R 28 27 26 25 24 23 22 21 20 19

Front: Kids taking a selfie
Back: Social media post

Find the Truth!

Everything you are about to read is true *except* for one of the sentences on this page.

Which one is **TRUE**?

T or F Twitter is the most widely used social media service.

T or F There are millions of fake accounts on the biggest social media services.

Find the answers in this book.

Contents

THE **BIG** TRUTH!

Fake Friends

username1

username1 These new shoes are the coolest! Everyone should get a pair.

Social media connects the world.

4 The Future of Social Media

How might social media continue
to grow and change? 33

Storage in
the cloud

username
Today

Can anyone teach me how to be safe and responsible online?

💙 45
👍 Like

5 Comments
💬 Comment

Many social media services require users to be at least 13 years old. Don't sign up for a site if you don't meet the age requirement! Instead, with your parent's or a trusted adult's permission, try finding one that is meant for kids. For example, Facebook and YouTube both have special kid-friendly versions.

Making Connections

Do you use a smartphone, tablet, computer, or video game system to post messages and chat with your friends? Do you share photos or watch videos online? If so, then you are one of the billions of people who use social media. Social media are services with apps and websites that allow users to create and share content with each other online. For countless people around the world, they play a huge role in everyday life.

Help Sam be smart about social media.

Many Types of Media

Social media can take many different forms. Some of the simplest ones, such as text chats and online message boards, have been around almost as long as the internet itself. But most of today's popular social media apps and sites were created in the 2000s or later. Before this time, most people used the internet to view content created by website owners. But since then, the internet has undergone a huge shift toward more **user-generated content**.

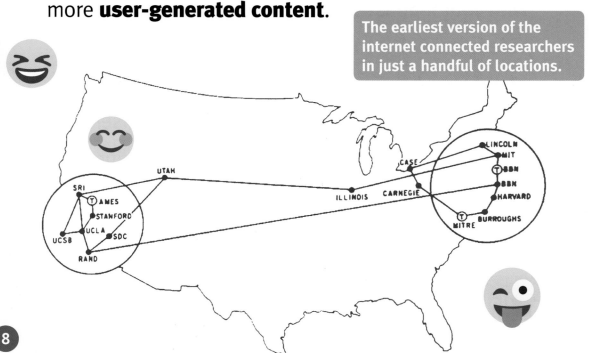

The earliest version of the internet connected researchers in just a handful of locations.

Each type of social media has its own purpose. For example, YouTube users can post videos for audiences around the world to watch and comment on. Instagram is a popular way to share and view photos. Blogs allow users to post their writings and receive feedback from readers. Social **networks** such as Facebook and Twitter allow people to create profiles, post short messages, share web links, and receive updates from their online followers.

YouTube

Instagram

Facebook

Twitter

Spreading the Word

News can travel fast online. When you post something on social media, other people are able to see it. If it is interesting, your followers will share it with their followers. Then those people will share it with even more people. Before long, millions of people might have seen the original post. This is called going viral.

Other times, lots of people online might start talking about the same topic all at once. This means the topic is trending. It often happens when a big news story breaks.

The Impact of ♥ Influencers

Some people have built audiences of thousands or even millions of followers on social media. They might make funny YouTube videos or post photos of exotic places on Instagram. They might have interesting things to say on Twitter, or they might just be celebrities who already have a lot of fans. Either way, many people are paying attention to these **influencers**. When a popular influencer posts something, it can go viral or start trending almost immediately.

Ethan Gamer is a social media influencer with millions of YouTube subscribers. These fans love watching Ethan's videos about popular games such as *Minecraft* and *Roblox*.

11

Pros and Cons

There are a lot of good things about social media. It is a great way to find new videos, music, and other fun content. It also helps people stay in touch with friends and relatives. You can send videos of your piano recital or basketball game to your grandparents in a different state. If your best friend moves away, you can chat or play games together online. Many people also use social media to make new friends who share their ideas and interests.

Social media is a great way to share an important event with people who couldn't be there to see it live.

Be careful not to post things that might make someone sad or hurt their reputation.

Unfortunately, social media also has some downsides. One issue is that the things you post can stay online for a long time. For example, you might accidentally post an embarrassing photo of yourself. Even if you delete the post, someone else might already have saved the photo. You could see it show up online again days, months, or even years later. Another problem is that people can use social media to hurt others. They can spread rumors, send insulting messages, or steal people's identities.

Each member of a development team brings unique skills to help the group.

According to the U.S. Bureau of Labor Statistics, about 163,000 Americans work as web developers.

CHAPTER 2

Apps, Websites, and More

The very best social media services seem simple when you first try them. They are easy to use, and most people don't need much help to get started with them. But building and operating a social media service is anything but easy. Huge teams of creative, skilled **developers** put a lot of hard work into creating the social media apps, websites, and other programs we use every day.

Talking to Computers

Like all computer programs, social media apps and websites are built using code. Code is a set of instructions for a computer that are written using a variety of **programming languages**. Most programming languages use a combination of words, phrases, symbols, and numbers. Like the languages people speak, each one has its own rules and grammar. Developers learn the ins and outs of programming languages and use them to create code that tells devices how to respond when you post or browse on social media.

Understanding programming languages can be a big help in a lot of careers.

More Than Just Good Looks

When you use social media, you do not actually see code. Instead, you interact with a user **interface** (UI). A UI consists of everything you see on screen while using social media. UI designers think carefully about how to arrange links, text boxes, and other interactive parts of an app or a website. They also consider how posts, user profiles, and other content should appear on your screen. These things can have a major effect on how easy and fun an app or a website is to use.

Button for more options

Profile picture and username

Ways to interact with this photo

username
Yesterday

I am still learning how to use this interface!

45   5 Comments
Like   Comment

Buttons, menus, and information are laid out carefully on a good interface.

A website or an app that loads too slowly can leave users feeling unhappy with the experience.

Staying Speedy

No one likes to use an app or a website that loads slowly or feels sluggish. To keep users from growing bored or frustrated with social media services, developers work hard to make sure their apps and sites are fast and responsive. This involves designing a good UI. It also requires developers to write **efficient** code. If a computer has to follow extra steps to get the desired results, it will take longer to complete an action.

Dealing With Devices

Think of all the devices you can use to access social media. There are countless types of phones, computers, tablets, and game systems available. Each one might have a different screen size. Some are faster and more powerful than others. Some have touch screens, while others do not. Developers have to make sure their services work equally well on all of these different devices. Doing this correctly involves careful attention to detail and a lot of testing.

Skilled designers make sure their work looks good on different devices. This is called responsive design.

Data Details

Whether you post new content, leave comments, update your profile, or simply browse, you create **data** when you use social media. This data is recorded in a database. A database is a collection of information that can be searched and sorted into different categories. Social media apps and websites rely on databases to customize each user's experience. For example, your Facebook posts are stored in Facebook's databases. When your friend logs in, Facebook finds your posts in its databases and displays them in your friend's feed.

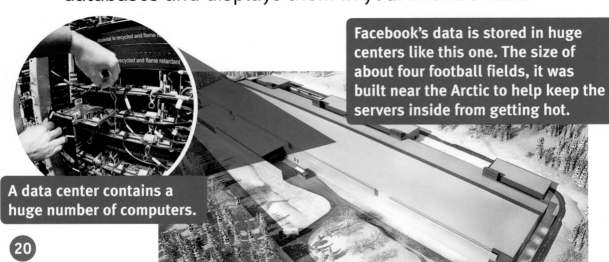

Facebook's data is stored in huge centers like this one. The size of about four football fields, it was built near the Arctic to help keep the servers inside from getting hot.

A data center contains a huge number of computers.

Floating in the Cloud

You can access the same social media account from any phone, computer, or other device. You can even log in on multiple devices at once and see all the same content. This is because social media services are based around cloud technology. Instead of storing information on users' devices, cloud services store their

Cloud technology makes it very convenient for users to manage their files and other information online.

data on computers called **servers**. When you log in, the app or website connects to the servers through the internet. This lets it access data that is stored far away from your device.

Millions of social media accounts are fake.

About two-thirds of all links posted on Twitter come from accounts run by computer programs instead of actual people.

CHAPTER 3

Digital Deception

Not everything you read or see online is true. Some people have learned that they can use social media to spread lies and misinformation. Many of them have gotten very good at it. Often, false information on social media is disguised as something that might seem trustworthy at first glance. Learning how to tell the difference between what's real and what's not is an important skill for anyone who uses social media.

Not Really News

One of the most common types of misinformation that spreads through social media is fake news. Fake news articles look a lot like real ones. But real news articles are carefully researched by journalists who support their writing with facts. Fake news articles purposely include untrue information and are designed to go viral. Always check the source when you read an article on social media. Does it come from a trusted newspaper or a well-known writer? Or is it just a post on a little-known website?

BREAKING NEWS
Aliens In Utah!

Sometimes fake news articles are exaggerated versions of true stories. Other times they are completely made up by their authors.

Phony Photos

Like real news articles, fake news stories are often accompanied by photos. A photo of something being described in an article makes the story seem more believable. But modern photo-editing software makes it easy to cut and paste pieces of photos together to make a realistic-looking image. So, for example, even though you might see a convincing photo of a celebrity or politician doing something embarrassing, it might not be real.

No Secrets on Social Media

The companies that run social media services can sometimes be dishonest or misleading, too. They are businesses, and their goal is to make money, not to keep their users safe. The main way most social media companies make money is by collecting as much information as possible about each and every user. Many people freely reveal their birth dates, hometowns, and other personal data on social media.

Online Communication Over the Years

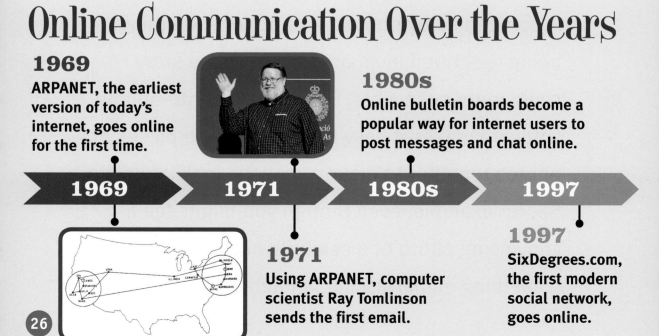

1969
ARPANET, the earliest version of today's internet, goes online for the first time.

1980s
Online bulletin boards become a popular way for internet users to post messages and chat online.

| 1969 | 1971 | 1980s | 1997 |

1971
Using ARPANET, computer scientist Ray Tomlinson sends the first email.

1997
SixDegrees.com, the first modern social network, goes online.

Social media services often use their users' data to sell advertisements. For example, a company might pay a social media service to run ads that will be seen by people who match certain categories. This is not necessarily a bad thing by itself. The problem is that social media companies do not always tell people how their data will be used. And sometimes they also fail to keep users' data safe from **hackers** or other threats.

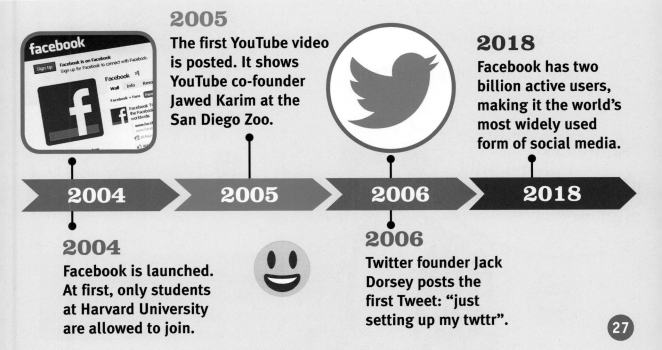

2005
The first YouTube video is posted. It shows YouTube co-founder Jawed Karim at the San Diego Zoo.

2018
Facebook has two billion active users, making it the world's most widely used form of social media.

2004 | **2005** | **2006** | **2018**

2004
Facebook is launched. At first, only students at Harvard University are allowed to join.

2006
Twitter founder Jack Dorsey posts the first Tweet: "just setting up my twttr".

Staying Safe

Just because there are some bad things about social media doesn't mean you shouldn't use it. As long as you follow a few basic safety rules, you can enjoy the benefits of social media without too much trouble. The first step is to avoid posting personal information online. Don't share your real name or where you live. Avoid using the name of your school. Be careful to avoid sharing other people's personal information, too.

username is at Greenville Middle School
June 30

Congratulations to my friends who just won our school championship tournament today!

♡♥ 20

👍 Like   2 Comments   💬 Comment

username2 Yikes! Now everyone knows where we go to school!

"Should I post this photo of my friends after their big win?"

Be extra careful about posting photos. They often contain personal information about you that you might not notice at first.

When you take a selfie with friends, be sure to ask before posting it online.

Beware of who you talk to on social media. Strangers online are no different than strangers in real life. People who seem nice might be trying to trick you.

Finally, always be considerate of others when you post online. Never send hurtful messages or talk about people behind their backs. You should also always ask permission before posting a photo or video of a friend, especially if it might be embarrassing in some way.

THE BIG TRUTH!

Fake Friends

Some social media accounts you see online do not represent actual people. They might have a real-sounding name and a photo of a real person as their profile picture. But people make fake accounts to hide their true identities. They might do this in order to trick people or break the law online. But more often, these fake accounts belong to bots.

Bots are computer programs that can automatically control social media accounts and make them perform various jobs, such as following other accounts or commenting on certain kinds of posts. A single person or organization might control thousands of bots at a time. Most of the time, the people controlling the bots are up to no good.

username3
Shared a post
Today

N! **BreakingNews!**
June 30 • 🌐

Aliens Land in Utah

10.9M Views

👍 Like   💬 Comment   ➡ Share
❤️ 200k   1,321 Comments

Bots often share links to fake news articles and even comment on the articles. Because bots often look like real accounts, this makes it look like lots of people are talking about the articles. Real people get drawn into the conversation and read the fake news.

When lots of people on social media start speaking out against unfair actions by a government or company, the organization being criticized might use bots to drown out the complaints. If enough bots are posting positive things, it might seem like there are only a few people who are unhappy.

username1

♥ ♡ ⊲ 🔖

username1 These new shoes are the coolest! Everyone should get a pair.

@username4

I'm tired of being treated this way by big companies!

Today 11:04 AM

102 Reposts   **54** Likes

💬   ⤺   ♡   ⤴

@username5
Enough is enough!

@username6
I don't see your point. You are overreacting.

@username7
I am tired of it, too! You could not have said it better!

The top social media influencers often get paid to post about products and companies. They need to keep their follower numbers high to keep making money. Sometimes they pay companies to make bots follow them, "like" their posts, or share their content so more people see it. This makes them seem more popular.

Many people use social media to record clips of concerts and other events so their friends can see what they're up to.

About 71% of all young adults (ages 18-24) in the United States use Snapchat multiple times each day.

CHAPTER **4**

The Future of Social Media

Though social media is a common, widely used way of sharing information, it is still new compared to most other forms of communication. This means everyone from lawmakers and developers to everyday users are still figuring out how exactly it should fit into our society. The world of social media has already seen many changes over its short history, and it is sure to keep changing in the coming years.

Even if you are careful with your account, the information you give to social media companies can still be stolen.

Stolen Data

One issue affecting the future of social media is privacy. In 2018, it was revealed that a company called Cambridge Analytica had managed to get around Facebook's privacy protection systems and collect the private information of tens of millions of Facebook users. The company knew who these Facebook users were, where they lived, and what kinds of interests they had, among other things. For the first time, many people realized that the information they post online every day is not truly private.

After news of the data leak broke, the U.S. Congress began investigating. Had Facebook done enough to keep users' data safe? Or was the leak a result of poor security? The event sparked a debate about whether the government should place more laws and restrictions on the way social media companies operate. Some people think it is the only way to keep users safe. Others argue that social media companies will learn from mistakes and do a better job of protecting their data.

Facebook founder Mark Zuckerberg testified before Congress about the Cambridge Analytica data leak.

Changing Opinions

The main reason Cambridge Analytica collected data from Facebook was to try to influence voters during the 2016 U.S. presidential election. By examining people's interests and personalities, it hoped to create articles and posts that would persuade different types of people to vote a certain way. It was not the only organization to use this technique during the election, either. During future elections, voters will need to work harder than ever to stay informed and avoid false stories about candidates.

Everyone Is Connected

One big advantage of social media is that it can bring people from all over the world together. This includes people who live in remote areas where there aren't a lot of chances to meet new people. A person living in a tiny, rural village can talk to the same people, watch the same videos, and listen to the same music as someone in the middle of a big city. People from distant countries can get together online to share ideas and work on projects together. Such an open exchange of information could lead to some amazing new inventions, artwork, and businesses in the future.

Friends around the world can stay in touch using social media.

A Louder Voice

Social media is also bringing a lot of positive changes that could have a huge effect on the future. Because social media is open to almost everyone, it is easier than ever for people to make themselves heard. Groups of students around the world have used social media to speak out against bullying, protest education budget cuts, and more. For example, in 2015, an 11-year-old girl used Twitter to collect and donate thousands of books.

A hashtag symbol (#) turns any word or group of words that directly follow it into a searchable link. Activists often use hashtags to spread awareness and build support for their causes.

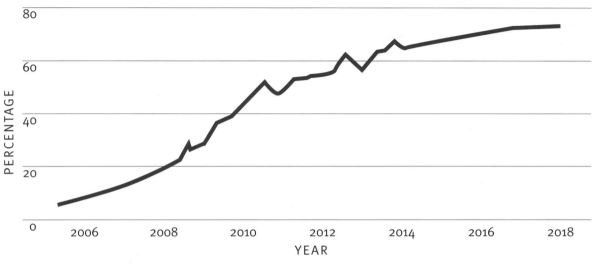

Percentage of U.S. adults who use at least one social media site

Source: Pew Research Center, surveys conducted 2005-2018

No Signs of Slowing Down

It's safe to say that social media is here to stay. The number of users on major social media services is continuing to grow. Many people have come to rely on it as their main way to stay in touch with friends and keep up with news. It is sure to remain a major part of our lives. Learning how to use it effectively and safely will provide necessary skills for the future. 😃

Spot the Problem

Take a look at these examples of social media posts. In each one, Sam has made a mistake and broken a rule for staying safe on social media. Can you spot the mistake in each post?

Help Sam solve these social media problems.

1

username

2

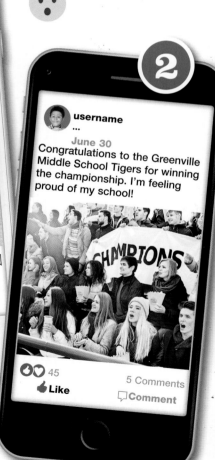

username
...
June 30
Congratulations to the Greenville Middle School Tigers for winning the championship. I'm feeling proud of my school!

45

Like   5 Comments   Comment

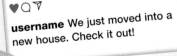
username We just moved into a new house. Check it out!

username8:
So, do you have a birthday coming up? When is it?

username:
Yeah! It's on May 16, and all my friends are coming to my house for a party.

3

LEVEL 88

♥ 100

$ 88888888

x 8.8   8888

Mission display HUD. Lorem ipsum dolor sit amet Ipsum donec iaculis nunc sit amet placerat

ANTI-PROTON GUN 1000   PLASMA MISSILE 50

username Did anyone see the shoes Thomas wore to school today? They were so ugly!

4

Did you spot the problems?

1. Don't post photos of your house online. Someone can use this information to figure out where you live.

2. The name of your school counts as personal information, so you shouldn't post it online. Knowing where you go to school every day could make it easy for someone to find you.

3. Never reveal personal information such as your birthday or your real name online, especially when talking to people you don't know in real life.

4. Never post hurtful things about other people online.

Sticky Situations

Look at each one of these situations and think about what you would do. You can also ask your friends and family what they think. Then look below to see if you chose the best way to handle the situation.

SITUATION 1

You get a group chat from a group of kids at your school. Everyone is using the chat to make fun of another kid in your class.

What should you do?

ANSWER: Don't join in the bullying. After all, you wouldn't like it if the kids at school were saying mean things online about you. Instead, tell a parent or other trusted adult what's going on.

SITUATION 2

At a birthday party, you snapped a funny photo of your friends who have cake all over their faces. You want to post the photo on social media.

What should you do?

ANSWER: Always ask permission before posting photos of someone else online, especially if they might be embarrassing. Pictures showing people's faces count as personal information.

SITUATION 3

A friend at school wants to use your tablet to play a game, but she needs your password.

What should you do?

ANSWER: Never share your password with anyone except a parent or another trusted adult. If someone has your password, they could see all of your personal information and make posts as you. This is why it is also important to create social media passwords that are hard to guess.

SITUATION 4

You hear about a cool new social media app, and you'd like to try it. But when you go to sign up, you see that it is only for people age 13 and over.

What should you do?

ANSWER: If you are under 13, you should not try to sign up. Social media services have rules like this to keep kids safe and keep them from seeing inappropriate content. Even if there is no age requirement to sign up, you should always ask permission from a parent or trusted adult first.

True Statistics

Percent of U.S. adults who use YouTube: 73

Percent of U.S. adults who use Facebook: 68

Number of fake accounts on Facebook: Up to 270 million

Price to purchase 1,000 fake Twitter followers: About $10

Number of people worldwide who logged into social networks in 2017: About 3 billion

Number of people whose Facebook data was leaked to Cambridge Analytica: About 87 million

Did you find the truth?

F Twitter is the most widely used social media service.

T There are millions of fake accounts on the biggest social media services.

Resources

Books

Cornwall, Phyllis. *Online Etiquette and Safety*. Ann Arbor, MI: Cherry Lake Publishing, 2011.

Gregory, Josh. *Apps: From Concept to Consumer*. New York: Children's Press, 2015.

Raatma, Lucia. *Social Networks*. Ann Arbor, MI: Cherry Lake Publishing, 2010.

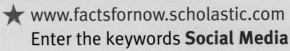

Visit this Scholastic website for more information on social media:

★ www.factsfornow.scholastic.com
Enter the keywords **Social Media**

Important Words

data (DAY-tuh) information collected in a place so that something can be done with it

developers (dih-VEL-uhp-urz) people who create software or build websites

efficient (ih-FISH-uhnt) working very well and not wasting time or energy

hackers (HAK-urz) people who have special skills for getting into computer systems without permission

influencers (IN-floo-uhns-urz) people who use their large social media followings to spread opinions and ideas

interface (IN-tur-fase) a system used to interact with a computer

networks (NET-wurks) groups of connected computers or communications equipment

programming languages (PROH-gram-ing LAYNG-gwij-iz) special languages used to create instructions for a computer to follow

servers (SUR-vurz) computers shared by two or more users in a network

user-generated content (YOO-zur JEN-uh-ray-tid KAHN-tent) text, videos, photos, and other things posted to social media by users

Index

Page numbers in **bold** indicate illustrations.

About the Author

Josh Gregory is the author of more than 125 books for young readers. He currently lives in Chicago, Illinois.